CW00471869

Trust
at Scale.

The Content Strategy,
for Creative People

Fed up of marketing not being your thing?

It's time to turn content into your superpower.

By Toby Moore

Contents

Welcome to
Trust at Scale

The aim of this book is to boost your productivity and creativity when it comes to planning innovative content.

I'll be taking you through some simple but highly effective strategies for structuring your time, getting the most out of short bursts of planned productivity and, of course, creating great content that works for you and your brand.

We'll unlock your creativity and knock some confidence into your ability to express yourself through content; all while remaining focused on building a truly meaningful relationship with your audience.
We'll be dividing our attention between four units (the 'Four Ps' as I call them):

1. **Purpose**
2. **Planning**
3. **Production**
4. **Promotion**

This is so you can hunker down and get to grips with each one in turn, allowing one to feed into the other. Breaking it down in this way creates efficiency and allows you to understand the content as you're creating it- which ultimately means you can utilise it more creatively and successfully.

Make sure you're set up with a notepad and pen and be aware that I'll be providing templates and tools for you to work with throughout (so maybe also make sure you have a decent amount of uninterrupted time, a beverage of your choice and are sitting comfortably).

About the Author

I'm Toby Moore, I'm a dad, entrepreneur and content strategist.

Throughout my career as a creative, I have been continually expected to be a *passionate* and *naturally talented* marketer. But the truth is, I am not. I actually find marketing quite boring.

But I love making things. As a child I would keep an invention book, where I would - in intricate detail - map out weird and wild contraptions. From dog walking machines and shrink rays, to self-cooling hats and housekeeping robots.

As I got older, I turned to more artistic faculties such as music, performance and writing. Which then as I entered into the world of work, eventually got beaten and bent into event organising and content marketing.

In my time at work, I have developed content strategies, community projects and conference programmes for companies in the FTSE100, global software providers, edgy startups and solo-business hippies.

I left my career lifestyle behind me in 2016 and - through various guises - have *worked as myself* ever since. But for a long time, this often looked like *'doing people's content marketing for them'*, because that is what many people had come to know as my craft and trade.

However, this came with a long-standing discomfort, as I was neither really interested in or particularly good at marketing. I always made **great content.** And I understood *how to market it*, but neither the energy nor the love was ever really there to want to actually do it.

So, I decided to change the rules that appeared to come with the territory of content. To create simpler ways of marketing that didn't have to suffer from the weighty complexity of tactics like SEO, PPC, SEM or whatever other TBS (Total Bullshit) acronyms we're all *expected to learn* in order to market our work.

Instead, I carved out a new path, one which focuses on creativity, knowledge and relationships, which is the stuff that *really* matters most when real people are involved.

The result of this work is now laid out for you in this book, for you to learn from and copy.

These days I am committed to unlocking creative freedom in myself and others. Marketing comes into it, but it's effortless.

Through my business Content Club, I consult other businesses on how to develop more people-centred content strategies.

Alongside that, I organise TEDxBrighton, one of the UK & Europe's longest running and largest TEDx events. I also teach leadership, entrepreneurship and public speaking to various institutions. And of course, I make things, such as; music, books and art.

I even helped to make another person. My daughter Emmy gives me more joy, energy and purpose than anything else in my life. Watching her develop her own sense of creativity is a deeply fulfilling experience.

I hope this intentionally short but very practical book, brings you some quick and powerful answers, and provides you with an alternative way of working, in order to **get your ideas, creativity and content out into the world**.

How This
Book Works

As I mentioned, this book will be split of the Four Ps:
Purpose, Planning, Production and Promotion.

I want to set a clear expectation as to how they work
together to help form your complete content strategy:

Purpose

I can't stress the importance of this enough. Understanding
how our content allows us to **build trust** with our audience
is vital. If our content isn't achieving this, then it isn't high-
quality content.

To make sure we're creating with purpose, we first need a
strong idea of our own identity and our approach to
authenticity. We then need a full understanding of our
audience; their wants, needs, questions and concerns. We
need to understand the relationship between us and our
ideal customer.

Without a true purpose in mind we can easily lose our way
and content can begin to unravel; missing the mark entirely.
That's why we'll start here and really bed in your
understanding of the purpose of your content before moving
on to Planning.

Planning

Once we fully understand the purpose of our content, we
then need to figure out how to come up with the great ideas
we need to deliver that amazing content.

We'll cover:

- How to research your audience
- How to create a reliable, trusted set of tools and processes to manage and catalogue your ideas
- What you need to put in place to see those ideas through to fruition

We'll also look at the different structures of what we create and learn how those different pieces of content can work together to create a content journey that encourages genuine engagement.

Production

By this point you'll have a clear understanding of what you want to create- you'll be buzzing with enthusiasm and be ready to get to work (or so I hope!).

This section will help you to underpin your approach to production; the tools and processes you need to have in place to create an efficient and effective creative process. No longer will you spend 6 weeks writing a singular blog post!

We won't be covering how to create great imagery or content for specific platforms- instead we'll be making sure you know when to finish that blog post, how to access content to make sure it hits all the educational, empathetic and emotional notes we need it to, and how to set yourself up for success in this stage of the process.

Promotion

Many of you may be familiar with the common process of coming up with a hundred ideas for content (usually in the shower or while waiting for tea to brew), eventually taking one of those ideas out of your brain and putting it down on paper before finally getting your laptop open and starting to work on it...

You then spend the next several weeks 'working on it' (which usually means mindless tweaking and procrastination as you try to build up the confidence to actually publish and promote your spellbinding piece of content gold). Finally, you hit publish and move on to your next content idea as quickly as possible.

And... nothing. The frustration at the lack of interest and engagement seeps in- after all, you spent weeks (if not months) researching, deliberating, redrafting, lovingly crafting that content... and for what?!

The step you missed was, of course, promotion. And it's not surprising- after torturing yourself over one piece of content for so long you were sick to death of it and didn't spend any time promoting it, preferring to move on to the next idea that piqued your interest instead.

In this part of the book, you will come to understand how you can use time, energy and process to make sure you have a reliable method for promoting your content once it's out there. Each piece should get the eyes and ears it deserves before leading your audience on in their customer journey- this is where we make sure that happens.

Chapter 1.
Purpose: Building Trust with Content

Welcome to our first expedition into Purpose!

We'll be kicking things off with a discussion around the purpose of content and how you can start to understand how we use that purpose to enable more effective engagement through our content.

So, what *is* the purpose of content?

Task: Take two mins to note down half a dozen answers to this question in the context of your business.

You've probably noted some responses along the lines of:

- Getting engagement
- Getting likes and comments
- Building relationships with people
- Educating people
- Becoming an authority in my field

All of the above are perfectly good answers but, in adherence to the framework I've created, there is one answer that sums it all up perfectly… content builds trust.

Trust is the fundamental emotion that your audience must feel within their relationship with you in order to create sales-like behaviour. It's the ultimate commercial goal of content.

Here's a little fable that proves the point.

Imagine that we're in some market in the Middle Ages- before the invention of iPhones, teletext, and even electricity. Imagine yourself walking in and buying crops to feed your family. There is only one farmer selling crops, so, the only person you can buy these crops from is this farmer, meaning you buy the crops no matter what price they are. What the farmer is competing on is availability; the availability of crops is what drives sales-like behaviour.

Now, let's say a couple of months go by and we walk into the market again- now there are two or three farmers selling crops. They're selling the same products from the same land, so what they need to compete on now is actually cost. Whoever's selling that same crop for the cheapest price is more likely to make sales.

Another couple of months go by and the market's starting to expand even more. Now there are many farmers selling a whole range of different crops. So, you walk into the market and look at each individual one- there's an abundance of availability. There's also a wide variety of costs for you to choose from, so that's no longer the deciding factor. Instead, you start looking at quality; whether you want the best of the best or if a basic ingredient will do- that is your new deciding factor.

Then we move into the fourth and final phase of this competitive myriad. This is where there is an abundance of farmers with an abundance of availability at a wide range of different prices and levels of quality. Now you, the consumer, have a great deal of choice at hand. You don't need to shop around too much to find different quality at different prices, so what you really need to start doing is building a relationship with the farmers themselves...

Are they a likable person? Do you trust them? Do you feel like they're going to turn up next week with the same quality of crop? Do you feel like if you went back and said, "Oh, well actually the crop wasn't so good.", are they going to honour the purchase and the relationship that you've created with them? Are they going to remember who you are? Are they going to make the effort to understand you in order to build trust with you?

A busy marketplace is reliant on trust. With a mass of competitors around you, what's going to underpin your customer base is how much trust you can build with them. That's their deciding factor in choosing you over all the alternatives.

Content will always be the strongest, most important tool when it comes to building trust. Outside of face-to-face interaction, it's the most effective way of replicating your personality, your approach to work and your knowledge (and generosity in sharing that knowledge)- while making it digestible for your ideal audience.

It's simple really. People buy from people, and in a saturated marketplace, they only buy from people they trust.

Building Trust Through Content

So how do we build trust through content alone?

First, we need to understand the power of our face-to-face interactions. The best way of selling during face-to-face interactions is to speak to people in a very human way. You need to meet them, talk to them, shake their hand, smile, joke, ask them genuine questions (and then actually *listen* to their answers) as that's what builds a relationship. That's what builds trust.

We then need to think about replicating this magic through our content. Every process needs to be geared towards it. Our creative process, planning strategies, the platforms we use and how we use them- all of this can be used to give us the best chance of replicating a great face-to-face encounter.

This will come up again later on, but for now it's something to mull over.

Chapter 2.
Purpose: Great Quality Content

In this section we're going to look at what defines 'quality' content and why it underpins the purpose of everything we create (we'll be focusing on the tools and processes we can use to quality-check our content a bit later on).

Why is quality so important? Because it builds trust.

How do we assess the quality of our content? Well, I like to approach it using the Three Es: Education, Empathy and Entertainment. Let's break down each one in more detail.

Education

This element is all about what you can teach your audience; what knowledge do you have that you can share? More importantly, what can you share most generously with them? What do they *want* to learn?

You need to stand out in the marketplace as an authoritative, knowledgeable figure, and sharing your knowledge freely and easily (instead of behind pay walls) builds trust and a sense of generosity. Some people worry about giving away knowledge (especially consultants, understandably), but let me put your mind at rest.

The fear is that your audience will use that knowledge to do your job for you and without paying you. But let's be honest, no amount of blog posts, 'top tips' or mini-guides are going to replace you and your years of experience.

You can use these drips of knowledge to show your audience your depth of understanding and the complexity of what you do- and there's no better advert than that. If anything, a window into your world will more likely convince your audience that they do *not* want to do the job themselves and that they better hand it over to you!

Empathy

For empathy to be apparent in your content, you first need an intimate understanding of the problems faced by your audience and the ambitions they may have. You also need to make that understanding clear through your language choices.

The reader should always feel like they are reading from their own perspective- challenges should be discussed as if you have experienced the same issue yourself. That way it comes across as something you share and understand, rather than something you might be accusing your audience of or exploiting a vulnerability they may have.

Entertainment

This doesn't refer to happiness, fun or excitement necessarily- I mean this more in terms of getting across the emotion and personality of the messaging you're trying to convey. If you think of it in terms of films, we can find entertainment in scary films, outrageous comedies and dramas in equal measure- they're all just different forms of entertainment.

Choosing your approach comes down to how you approach face-to-face interactions with your target audience- your style there should be reflected in your content creation. What are you doing to build intimate trust with someone in a business environment or a selling environment? What personality qualities work best for you? If you can narrow down a few qualities you bring to the table when selling face-to-face, you can focus on channelling these into your content through tone of voice, design, structure etc.

When creating our content, there should always be a proportionate dose of all three Es.

Building a Content Strategy Mission Statement

A really important element of the trust-building tool kit is to have a purpose statement for your entire content strategy. A great purpose statement will act as your consistent True North, acting as a guide for decision making and keeping you firmly on track.

Let me run you through a useful process for determining your content purpose statement: the WOC tool.

- **Who:** *"We help xyz…"*
- **Outcome:** *"To achieve xyz…"*
- **Content:** *"By creating xyz."*

You can fill in the blanks for yourself- start now and jot down some ideas. My responses are below for some guidance:

- **Who:** We help business owners and marketers who are trying to create better content when handling their own marketing.
- **Outcome:** We want them to become more confident, productive content creators.
- **Content:** By creating educational tools, workshops and training materials.

So, at Content Club, we help business owners and marketers to become more confident, productive content makers by creating educational tools, workshops and training materials. Simple.

Hopefully that exercise has given you some clarity and a great purpose statement for you to come back to, whenever your work starts to wonder...

Chapter 3
Purpose: Goals & Objectives

In this last section of 'purpose', we're going to look at goals and objectives around the content you're creating.

Quite commonly in marketing, we're taught that each piece of content has to have a clear call to action. This might be clicking through to a link for additional reading, downloading something or signing up to a mailing list etc.

It's always important to make sure that you include a call to action in your content, however, if you really want to proactively build relationships and trust, you need to use a call to *conversation*.

Creating a Call to Conversation

A call to conversation is very different from a call to action.

Action is something you're not personally involved with, whereas a call to conversation starts to move the person engaging with your content into a place where they enact sales behaviour through building trust and a genuine relationship with you.

A simple example might be posting something on social media and asking people for their opinion: *"I've been working on this content, how do you think I should move forward with X, Y and Z?"* Or if you're offering a download, instead of approaching it as *"Go and fill in the form to get the download"*, an alternative as a call to conversation might be, *"If you would like to receive this piece of content I've been working on, send me a direct message or comment below."*

Instantly, you can see that you're creating a conversation on a one-to-one basis as a result of someone engaging with your content.

Content Objectives

Let's look at this in terms of how different brands, products and services operate.

The Content Objective Chart has 4 quadrants:

- Selling Products Online
- Traffic, Reach and Engagement
- Creating Conversations
- Demonstrate What I Can Do

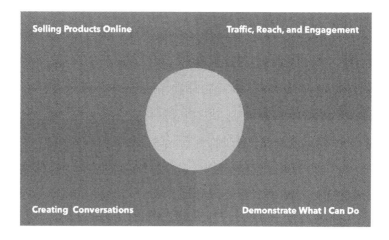

Selling Products Online

Typically, this is where eCommerce brands sit. If you sell products online, embedding calls to action in your content is

17

more effective because your goal is to push people from building up knowledge around your product and brand, to them buying from your online store.

Traffic, Reach and Engagement

Calls to action are very important here too because this is where you'll find news brands, influencers and monetised content brands. They're less interested in building relationships and more interested in measurable metrics (such as 'likes', clicks, and comments) which demonstrate value to sponsors and advertisers.

Creating Conversations and Demonstrate What I Can Do

In these two quadrants, we're looking at scalable products and services such as subscriptions as well as consultancy, freelance and one-to-one services. With these, you need to be creating conversations and using your content to demonstrate your knowledge, experience and most importantly, what it *feels like* to work with you.

Swapping out your calls to action for 'calls to conversation' in the tops and tails of your content is going to be much more effective here. For example, inviting people to message you, complete a survey or ask a question in the comments.

Example: Eve Mattresses

One of my first clients was Eve Mattresses. At the time, they were a very disruptive brand; mattresses are very commoditised products, and they were actively trying to de-commoditise them.

You might think that one of their competitors is Dreams Mattresses with both of them selling mattresses online, surely they're operating in the same way? But actually their sales, marketing content and social media strategies were radically different.

Dreams want you to buy a mattress and come back when you need a new one, making it eCommerce led. They're not trying to create a conversation with you- they just want you to see them as the most affordable option. Earlier in our guide, we looked at the different maturities of selling in terms of availability, cost, quality and trust- commoditized brands are sitting in the cost and quality bracket.

If you were to mature to a higher price point, like Eve, where they're selling the cheapest mattress for around £700, then you need to think about how you're going to build relationships and trust. You don't just buy the mattress because it's just a great mattress. You buy it because you love the brand and the real personality that comes through in their content.

There's a very conscious approach to creating a conversational, accessible, likeable and trustworthy brand. It's only ever achieved by understanding how you replicate those qualities in your content and how you use that content to create conversations- allowing your audience to engage so you can nurture them into customers.

Call to Action or Call to Conversation?

So, which quadrant do you think your brand sits in within the Content Objective Chart?

Take 60 seconds to think about it.

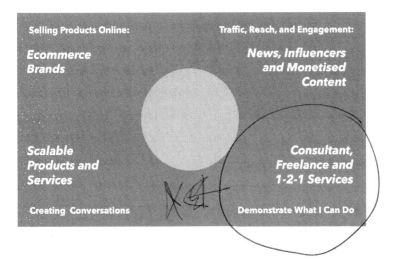

Hopefully you didn't choose the white spot in the middle, because that is the danger zone and an indecisive place to be. One of the most important qualities that you can have as a business owner, content creator or marketeer is to make conscious and decisive decisions about the purpose of your content.

When you know where you want to be, you can create content as individual pieces and then decide whether you have a call to action and push people through to buying something or a call to conversation where you create the opportunity to build relationships and trust with people.

Chapter 4
Planning: Journeys & Categories

As we're now in the planning section of our guide, we're going to be looking at some of the tools, techniques and processes you can utilise to effectively plan, ideate, and create your content.

We'll be taking a flexible approach that can be adjusted to fit in with the time and energy you have available to you, as well as the needs of your audience.

We're going to start off by looking at some of the content journeys we can create for audiences- thinking logically about how we structure our content, the relationships between different kinds of content and how we define the types of content that we create.

Categories of Content

I want to start by highlighting the 3 main categories of content that you should be working with:

- **Core content**
- **Supporting content**
- **Promotional content**

Concept

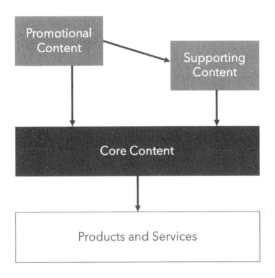

Example

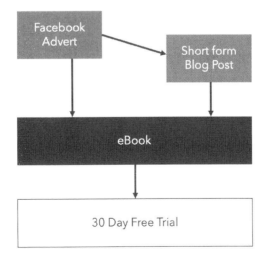

22

By utilising each of these categories, we're ensuring that we're fulfilling each necessary stage of the audience journey- from discovering the company/product to ultimately becoming customers.

Core Content

This content is essentially going to drive sales-like behaviour. That is its purpose.

This can look very different from one brand to the next, but typical examples would be a downloadable e-book, a webinar that you're inviting people to take part in or a podcast that leads people through to various services and products that they can buy.

As you can see, usually there is some sort of transaction involved- that could be a data transaction (such as an email address, filling in a contact form or making a phone call) or a financial transaction (such as selling an e-book or a physical low-cost item that may indicate a strong potential for further, more valuable transactions further down the line).

The key with core content is to ensure that what you are 'selling' is genuinely of high value to your customer. It should be something that heavily documents your knowledge, is highly educational and shows off your expertise.

It should also be something with a long shelf life- it needs to sit comfortably in your catalogue of content across your website and social media channels for the foreseeable future and be evergreen in its appeal to your target market.

It's also key to consider where you want to display it- core content is not something to be lost in 24 hours on Twitter.

Maybe it would sit better on a well-tested landing page on your website so that you can own the space and not fall foul of any inevitable changes to social media platforms or algorithms etc.

Ideally, you want to own the platform that your core content is on, and you want to make sure that you can manage and measure the transactions going on there too.

As a vital part of your strategy, core content should be first on your list. It should be planned first so we can then chop it up and turn it into supporting and promotional content.

Supporting Content

Supporting content is created with the aim of building trust within your audience.

Most people will need a little persuasion to become a customer (despite your clearly awesome core content). They may need to be nurtured through a dozen or more pieces of supporting content before they're ready to move into the sales-like headspace required for your core content to be effective.

Supporting content should be bite size; something that can be digested in around 5 mins, with a high value-transfer. Examples would be short-form blogs, videos and newsletters.

This content should also have a decent shelf-life, be very easy to engage with and to produce with some regularity e.g. a blog every 2-4 weeks, a video every 4-6 weeks etc.

Promotional Content

So, we've got Core Content at the top (something you make once and get as much value from as you can), Supporting Content in the middle (where you're creating regular engagement to nurture trust and build a relationship), and then, we have Promotional Content.

This has a shorter shelf-life, even 24 hours in some cases- which means you have to make the most of the content within its lifespan.

It's largely there to allow potential customers to discover you and to move them on to the next stage of the process i.e. towards the Supporting or Core content you have produced (depending on what you're trying to achieve- there's nothing wrong with skipping over Supporting Content and on to the juicy Core stuff if your Promotional content is compelling enough to allow for it).

The most obvious platform for Promotional content is social media; Twitter, Facebook, Instagram- wherever your audience is most likely to be and where you can create content that's very quick and easy to engage with.

This content should be entertaining; highlighting your personality and emotional qualities over and above any educational aspects- that side of things is taken care of later in the customer journey.

What you want to do with Promotional content is create the *promise* of learning and value.

It should be high energy:

"Hey guys, I'm here, I'm doing this, I'm just like you and we should have a relationship and we should build trust with each other. If you want to continue this and do more, why don't you go read my blog? Why don't you watch this great video? Why don't you download this thing and learn more?"

That's the kind of behaviour you're trying to drive through Promotional content.

Once you've successfully lined up your three layers of content, you can then channel your audience through to your products and services by, for example, offering a free trial-help them to take each step in the journey.

Chapter 5
Planning: Content Types

If content categories are the functional elements of the content journey, content types are the individual blocks that we fulfil those categories with. For example: a short-form blog post, a 30-second video, a LinkedIn post or a landing page.

We want to create clear definitions around these content types so that the difficult decisions around what the content will look like and what platform the content will be posted on are made early on. This way, when the creative process comes around, all you need to focus on is creating a great piece of content.

Your Current Content Types

Take a few minutes to write down which content types you're already using. During this process, you might find that you're actually creating a lot more content than you thought.

Now, let's create some constraints around this. If you had to choose only 3 content types to move forward with, what would they be? Circle these on your piece of paper.

For argument's sake, let's say you've selected short-form blogs, 30-second videos and an eBook...

Fitting These into Your Categories

Short-form blogs are supporting content. You might be creating these blogs once a month, posting them on your website and then re-promoting them on social media platforms.

30-second videos are promotional content. They're quick to consume as well as fun to make and engage with. It's very easy to push people from a short and consumable piece of content through to something more nurturing, like a blog post.

In the journey, that video will look like something like:

"I've just published this amazing new blog post. If you'd like to check it out, go and read it."

Followed by your blog which has a conversational tone much like...

"Here's some really interesting educational material. You and I are the same. When you encountered this problem, what did you do? Here are the three ideas I used to solve the problem."

And the last piece (your eBook) is the core content. This could be a downloadable guide which is a collection of blog posts, or you might do it the other way around. You create an eBook and then chop it up into blog posts, which forms the inspiration for your videos.

From here, you can see that we've taken a really effective route to manage the journey that your audience is going on by making sure that all your content is clearly related. Alongside this, we're also making sure that the creative process is as efficient as possible by repurposing ideas and materials through different content types.

The reality is that you'll probably be working with more than 3 content types because your audience is going to be found on various platforms, so you need to make sure that your content is tailored.

Content Types Planner Sheet

Using the Content Types Planner Sheet, create a content type for each category - core content, supporting content and promotional content. So, you need to define:

- Type of content
- Format
- Length
- Images
- How often you will create this piece of content
- Whether it will have a call to action or call to conversation

This activity will help you to visualise what your content strategy will look like, meaning you can now start to move the components from this planner into the content journey that you want to create.

(*template on next page*)

CORE	SUPPORTING	PROMOTIONAL
Content Type *(Eg. eBooks, or Webinars)*	Content Type *(Eg. Blogs or short videos)*	Content Type *(Eg. Facebook posts or Tweets)*
Format *(Eg. 2000 words, PDF, 10 pages, + photos)*	Format	Format
How often will you make this? *(Eg. weekly, daily)*	How often will you make this?	How often will you make this?
CTA - Call to action *(Eg. Buy now, read more, message me!)*	CTA	CTA

Chapter 6
Planning: Ideas for Content

Next on our list are Audience Personas- a vital step in planning out your content as it ensures you're targeting the right people. We're can use your personas as a catalyst for building a catalogue of focused ideas and topics for content moving forward.

Building a Content Persona

If you've ever built a marketing or customer persona before then you will be familiar with the process but, for those among us who are new to the concept, the idea is to build a picture of your target demographic through the persona of a single character, to deepen your understanding of their wants and needs. This enables you to tailor your product and/or services to suit and to market them in the best way possible to suit your audience.

As we're focused on content creation, we will be going a level deeper and concentrating on asking:

a) What questions may your audience persona have?
b) What questions do we want to ask them?
c) How can we utilise the above to tailor our content?

There are 3 approaches you can take to understand your audience better, the first one being market research. This involves surveying our target market to get a better picture of their needs so that we can create content that meets those needs. Simple really!

The second approach is more SEO/technology-led; digging into Google Analytics, social media stats, search terms etc. with the goal of finding out what your audience are looking for and, most importantly, engaging with. This approach is based on cold, hard numbers and any content you create is led by those figures (typically resulting in an SEO-based strategy where you're in the race to the top of page one of Google). This can be a very expensive process and takes up so much time, energy and resources that we're not actually going to explore it any further here.

The third (far more human-led) option focusses more on your existing knowledge; your experience as the person that runs your business! Most likely you have a wealth of knowledge and a decent customer base to study- why not start with understanding and utilising what you already have?

This is by far the quickest route to understanding what questions and problems your audience persona is going to have, as well as how you're going to use content to meet those needs.

Using the Audience Persona Template

Because we're nice people, we've created a template for you to use when building a picture of your audience persona:

(*template on next page*)

As you can see, there are a number of different boxes for you to fill in and even space for an image. This may seem a bit ridiculous, but thinking of your audience as a singular, real entity can help focus your efforts.

So, as an example, I'm going to go ahead and name my persona Harriet.

Name: *Harriet*	Platforms: Others:	Questions they have *(these drive your ideas)*:
Picture:		1. *Where can I find new customers?*
		2. *Where can I be inspired for new graphic design ideas?*
		3. *How can I price up new projects for clients that I've not worked with before?*
		4.
		5.
Age Range: 20 to 25	Who do they already trust online?	Questions you would like to ask them *(these drive your CTA/CTCs)*:
		1.
Job: *Freelance Graphic Designer*		2.
		3.

Harriet is 22 years old and is a Freelance Graphic Designer by trade. She uses LinkedIn, Instagram and Facebook in order to a) be inspired for her own work and b) to then go and look out for new customers and collaborations.

In terms of who she trusts online, Harriet is connected with network of other Graphic Designers via Facebook and Instagram. She trusts them and the content that they create. She's also subscribed to a couple of industry publications that she believes in and trusts.

On to the questions Harriet has.

In her case these could be questions like:

- Where can I find new customers?
- Where can I be inspired for new graphic design ideas?
- How can I price up new projects for clients that I've not worked with before?

If you're struggling with this section, think about the existing customers that you have and the questions they ask you on a regular basis. In those first few days and weeks of your customer relationship, what questions are they coming to you with? What help and support do they need? I bet you'll think of more than five!

I'd advise you to take the time to fill out the template to this point right now and we'll come back to the questions we would like to ask them a little later. Don't over-think it; maybe set yourself a timer for 3 mins and crack on. Bonus points for excellent artistry when sketching the photo!

Using Your Audience Persona to Complete Your Topic Planner

So, now you've completed the majority of your Audience Persona template, we have another task for you: completing your Idea Planner (template below- yep I'm that good to you!).

Taking the 5 questions you've come up with for your Audience Persona to ask of you, humour me and just ask them out loud...Hearing the questions vocalised should really get them into your mind.

The next step is to move those questions across to the Topic Planner (using the boxes along the top) so we can use them as topics to underpin our content strategy and to create valuable content around them.

Using the headline ideas columns, you can come up with 5 answers to each of the questions which will then give you 25 content ideas. Using three or four content types, those ideas could cover your content calendar for a year- not bad for a half hour exercise!

Effectively this exercise gives you an edge. It allows you to create a content catalogue, so you don't need to constantly come up with ideas in a disjointed, frenetic way. You simply look back at your planner, pick an idea, marry it with the most suitable content type for your overall strategy and away you go.

To go back to our Harriet example, one of her questions was **'where can I find new customers?'.** One of my answers to that question may have been to try out new marketing platforms- so I can then create a blog, a short video and/or a small downloadable guide to fulfil that need.

Q1	Q2	Q3	Q4	Q5
Headline Ideas:	**Headline Ideas:**	**Headline Ideas:**	**Headline Ideas:**	**Headline Ideas:**
1	1	1	1	1
2	2	2	2	2
3	3	3	3	3
4	4	4	4	4
5	5	5	5	5

Your various forms of content lead your audience through a content journey and, hopefully, right into the palm of your hand. The breadcrumbs allow Harriet to start building a relationship with me so that she may want to find out what other products and services I have on offer that can help her in her personal quest to be the best Graphic Designer she can be.

I find this tool incredibly useful and will preach it to anyone who'll listen. It allows you to test your content ideas against the questions your Audience Persona is actually asking.

Top Tip: Trello

For anyone who's never heard of, seen or used Trello before, it's a free, user-friendly project planning tool (I'm not affiliated or sponsored, promise!).

I use a Trello board as my Topic Planner so I can access it anywhere and do my one hour per week of content planning whenever it suits. I move say 3 ideas across to my to-do list, make some basic notes for each one and it's then there waiting for me when I actually sit down to create later in the week.

This is a great way to manage your time and productivity as a content creator- diarise planning, productive and creative time every week to make sure you're always moving forward. I also recommend making time for promotion and engagement throughout the week too.

So, before you start scratching your head and working out which blog you're going to create next, make sure you go through this exercise and get some really great ideas down. Ones that are tried and tested against your audience persona (and your purpose statement too).

Chapter 7
Production: Creating Great Content

You've made it through the planning section of our guide! Welcome to chapter 7. From here we'll be moving on to the production side of things including processes and templates you can use to become more effective and productive in the creation of your content.

Content Quality Planner

For this we will be referring to the 3 Es we talked about in Chapter 2 - these are the foundations of great quality content:

1. **Education:** Knowing what you can teach, what your audience wants to learn and being generous with your knowledge.

2. **Empathy:** Understanding the challenges faced by your audience and showing that you've shared and overcome those challenges yourself.

3. **Entertainment:** Making sure your personality and the intended emotion behind the content comes across just as they would in a face-to-face interaction.

What Makes Your Content Great?		
Education Five things you can teach people	**Empathy** Five problems you can understand	**Entertainment** Five qualities you have
1.	1.	1.
2.	2.	2.
3.	3.	3.
4	4	4
5.	5.	5.

Education

You can use the template above to firstly outline 5 ideas for what you can *teach* your audience:

How'd you get on? Remember, these are living, breathing documents- not ideas to set in stone. You can deviate in the future by repeating the process as things evolve, and don't worry if it's looking a bit sparse for you at the moment- focus more on understanding the process and the framework so you can put it to good use as things become clearer.

If you happen to be smashing this, you'll hopefully see that the questions and answers we came up with during the audience persona exercise hang together nicely with what you've noted down here.

Empathy

Moving on to the empathy column- this is an interesting one as it's not just about *what* we're talking about but also the language we use.

Let's start with what we're talking about: your content topics should focus on the issues and ambitions of your target audience.

For example, a problem your audience may be facing could be that they're struggling to make sales online and here you are, ready to solve their problem through the products and services that you offer. So how are you going to talk about that problem? Your language needs to help build a connection and a shared sense of problem-solving with your audience.

There are a couple of ways you can approach this- one builds empathy beautifully, the other really doesn't. Here's a comparison for you:

> *"Do you think running your business would be easier if you could find quicker ways to meet new customers online?"*

> vs

> *"Finding new customers online is easy, you're just not thinking about it correctly."*

Both sentences lead to the same piece of content that would teach the same thing, but they're radically different in their approach to describing both the problem and the ambition.

The second uses a 'me vs you', accusatory approach to get the point across- not ideal for creating a sense of empathy! The reader may feel that their vulnerability is being exploited when reading the second example, rather than getting a sense that you're trying to enable them to reach their potential. Ultimately, this language choice could lead you to a few members of your audience, but it won't connect you with those who have the strength and ambition to become a quality customer.

Instead, remember that you're in the business of helping people. You most likely created your product or service in response to an issue you faced yourself- so come at it from this angle instead. Talk about the issue from a shared perspective: *"Isn't it frustrating when problem XYZ comes up and you don't know how to solve it? Luckily, I've been through this before and I'd really like to share my experience of solving the issue with you."*

With all that in mind, take a few minutes to fill in the Empathy column with 5 problems that you understand and can connect with your audience over.

They don't have to be problems that you can necessarily solve- just ones you feel confident in discussing and sharing real, honest experiences of.

Entertainment

Our final column covers 'entertainment'. As discussed in chapter 2, this doesn't necessarily mean being fun and exciting- it's more about getting your personality and emotions across through your content in as similar a way as possible to a face-to-face interaction.

People buy from people and, regardless of product or service, people will often buy from whoever feels like the best personality fit for them. So, the best approach is to meet and greet people, welcoming them into your business using content that matches your personality so you can build a genuine, authentic relationship.

Note: Don't be tempted to waste time and money trying to dupe your audience here- if they get to the point of being a buying customer, they will soon realise you're not who they thought you were, you'll lose them as a customer and the process will start again with someone else- a futile exercise for all parties!

So, again, take a few minutes to fill out the final column with 5 personality traits that best represent your face-to-face interactions with your customers.

If you get stuck, it can help to think about a person you've enjoyed working with recently or have had a great customer relationship with- what behaviours did you embody during your interactions? What were you doing with your face? Were you asking questions? Were you listening to what they were saying?

My completed **Content Quality Planner** is below as an example to anyone struggling, or just for the sake of interest:

(*Complete template is just beyond the next page*).

So, what you should be looking at now is a toolkit for defining what great quality content is for you and your brand. You may not refer back to this every single time you create a piece of content, but it's a great checklist to fall back on if you're losing confidence in an idea or if you're looking for direction on how to bring more life, energy and value into a piece of content.

Just by writing these guidelines down you'll probably find that your future content will naturally embody more and more of your quality planner. It's important to come back to it on a regular basis just to sense-check what you're producing.

- Does it meet the educational qualities that you've set out?

- Are you really discussing problems and ambitions, using language that empathizes with your audience, or are you taking cheeky shortcuts as a way of trying to make quick sales?

- Are you really embodying the personality and the tone of voice that you've laid out for yourself? Or are you trying to be something you're not in order to meet some imaginary need that you think your audiences has?

The chances are, if you can simply put the very best version of yourself out there in the content that you're creating then you will meet the right people, they will develop the right view of you and you will create meaningful, trustworthy and fruitful relationships with them.

(*Complete template on the next page*).

What Makes Your Content Great?

Education

Five things you can teach people

1. How to write a content plan

2. How to design content templates

3. How to use Facebook adverts

4. How to create video content

5. How to hire freelancers

Empathy

Five problems you can understand

1. That planning content is difficult

2. That content creation can become expensive

3. It's difficult to be consistent with content

4. It can be hard to come up with good ideas for new content

5. It is difficult to know how to create conversations online

Entertainment

Five qualities you have

1. I laugh and smile

2. I ask a lot of questions

3. I find out what people have tried already

4. I never TELL people what to do

5. I believe every problem can be solved.

Chapter 8
Production: Building Content Templates

Here we'll be looking at building a content template, which is probably the most valuable tool you can provide yourself with as a content creator.

Building content templates is an effective way of streamlining the creative process; allowing you to make important and decisive decisions around the content you want to create. Think of it as a catalogue you can pull off the shelf at any time.

What are Content Templates?

Let's say we're planning on writing a blog. Using the Content Template, we would plan that the blog will have 600 words, 4 headings and 2 calls to action/conversation.

We would then define the word count for each section of the blog as well as the purpose it's going to serve: the first 100 words will introduce the idea, the next 200 words will explain why this idea is important and the last 300 words will explain how the reader can put this idea into action, followed by a call to action or conversation that leads through to the next piece.

What if we were writing an eBook? Typically, we would aim for around 2000 words across 10 pages, with plenty of rich images. The first 2 chapters will set the scene, the next 3 will explain common challenges or problems and the final 2 will provide solutions. We would then have an outro page,

defining how our products and services can help the reader move forward with what is discussed in the eBook.
Here are some examples...

Short form Blog

600 words
4 headings
2 CTAs

Intro - **100 words**

What **is the idea? - 100 words**

Why **is useful - 200 words**

How **do you do it - 300 words**

CTA: **Download our eBook**

eBook

2000 words
10 pages
10+ images

About the eBook

2 chapters **Setting the scene**

3 chapters **explain common challenges**

2 chapters **giving answers**

1 outro **explaining other services (CTA)**

Remember, you can create templates for any type of content (e.g. videos, webinars and so on). Doing so will allow you to dictate what your parameters will be through templates, types and categories, allowing you to completely turbocharge and streamline the creative process through an efficient shortcut.

Take a few minutes to look at the Blog Template and think about what your version would look like based on some of the ideas you've come up with earlier in this guide.

(Template on next page)

Now, think about the categories and types you've come up with, how many templates you will need and what parameters you need to put into place to help you make the best decisions. We typically find that parameters around length, word count, images etc are useful to define beforehand.

At the start of this guide, we spoke about breaking up your time and energy into chunks. You want to put time aside for planning, ideation, maturing your audience personas and so on. Then there's also time set aside for production and promotion, with the production part being template creation.

Once you've got your templates in place, you need to be strict with yourself- make sure that you're efficient, effective and productive in your content creation. Think, *"I'm not going to create a piece of content unless I've got a template to base it on."* and stick to that rule.

As a next step, we want to look at where our templates correlate with the content types and frequencies we want to set.

Frequency is deciding how often we are going to create and promote a piece of content, Content Type (Chapter 5) is looking at the platforms we're using in terms of the goals we want it to achieve, and Categories highlight the purpose of that content within our content strategy.

Heading/Title:	Intro:		
What: 20% (e.g. 200/1000 words)	Why: – 30% (e.g. 300/1000 words)		
How: 50% (e.g. 500/1000 words) 1. Step one:	2. Step two:	3. Step three:	
Conclusion:	CTAs, CTCs, Links and Keywords:		

Finally, our templates help to define what our content will look like and what sort of assets we need to populate that content with. We will cover the One Page Planner at the very end of our guide, which explains how we fit all our ideas onto one page.

Take a few minutes to start making a short list of templates you think you should start building.

Visualise what your workweek might look like when you sit down on a, say, Wednesday afternoon to create content. You can quite simply pull an idea and template off the shelf, put them together and create a great piece of content in a very short space of time.

Chapter 9
Promotion: Platforms & Channels

We've spoken about the purpose of our content, planning ideas and how it fits in with our audience, understanding our creative process and putting templates in place to make sure our production is airtight. Now, we want to look at promoting our content.

Typically, promotion is left to the last minute and, sometimes, it's not covered at all. We publish content online and let the promotion look after itself- that's when we get frustrated weeks and months later because no one has engaged with our content, visited our landing pages or bought our products and services.

We really need to think carefully about how we create time and capacity to promote content. If we're putting lots of energy into creating something but then not working hard to share it, we've wasted time and that can be seriously demotivating.

So planning, producing and promoting need to be focussed on in equal measure. For promotion, we need to put some simple, actionable and manageable tasks in place.

First, let's talk about how we select the platforms and channels we're going to utilise for our content. We might just be using our own website, Facebook and Instagram because that's all we have time for. We want to focus on creating great quality engagements and, if we're spreading ourselves too thinly across different platforms, we can't give it the attention that it needs.

Make it Manageable

Whatever you choose to do, it has to be manageable. If you're just one person or a very small team, your strategy should reflect that. It can be so demotivating if we bite off more than we can chew, inevitably fail and then have to re-energise and try again.

Ask yourself- can I pull this off? Do I have enough time in my week or month?

It's much more effective to give yourself less to do to begin with and then to build up as and when it's possible.

Revisit Your Audience Persona

Revisit the audience persona you created in the planning section of our guide and start to understand how you came up with this, which platforms you identified as in use by your audience and how you can work this into the process of selecting platforms and channels.

So, if you produced 3 audience personas and Instagram was on all of them, you'd need to make sure that Instagram was on your platform planner.

Platform Planner

In the Platform Planner, you can see:

- Platform Name - e.g. Facebook
- Purpose to My Business - e.g. building and engaging with a community
- Who Can I Reach - e.g. communities and groups
- Content Types - e.g. articles, news and videos
- My Ability to Use (from a scale of 1-10, with 10 being really confident) - e.g. 9

As another example, let's look at Pinterest. You might not be very familiar with Pinterest but you know your audience use it as they're visual thinkers. It's an opportunity to reach potential customers and your content types would be photos, videos and articles that have a visually striking impact. The problem is, you've not used Pinterest before, and your lack of confidence is stopping you from moving forward.

You do have experience and therefore confidence in using email newsletters, but you can see that the value of email to your business is a lot less significant than Pinterest so... maybe it's time to consider upskilling.

(*template on the next page*)

Using the Platform Planner is a great process to go through- it can help you understand the value of a platform, your ability to use it and where your skill gaps might be.

Take a few minutes to fill this out with 3 or 4 platforms you want to include in your strategy, whilst also considering the audience personas, content categories and types.

This should give you a clear picture of the platforms and channels you have available, where you think your audience is and how you think you can leverage your strengths around creating content for those platforms to reach that audience.

A great outcome from this process is deciding *not* to use a specific platform. Many brands use certain platforms for the sake of it- mainly because they're comfortable with them. Look at your Platform Planner and see if anything emerges that will help you make the decision to remove a platform. If you can reduce the number of platforms you're marketing on, it allows you to create better quality content.

Platform E.g. Facebook groups	Platform	Platform	Platform	Platform
Purpose to my business e.g. Maintain engagement with customers community	Purpose to my business	Purpose to my business	Purpose to my business	Purpose to my business
Who can I reach e.g. Community members	Who can I reach	Who can I reach	Who can I reach	Who can I reach
Content Types e.g. Posts, Videos, Polls and Lives	Content Types	Content Types	Content Types	Content Types
My ability to use 7 /10	My ability to use /10	My ability to use /10	My ability to use /10	My ability to use /10

54

This task may also highlight any gaps in your coverage. So, if the 3 or 4 platforms that you've chosen are all very visual and there's nothing really text-based, and your audience is going to want written content to make decisions, it's going to help you realise that there's a gap in your content creation.

What platform could you potentially use to promote more written content? Is it your website? Or perhaps it's Medium or LinkedIn as they have great blogging tools built into them and a ready to reach audience?

Chapter 10
Promotion: Promotional Checklists

In this, the last part of the promotion section, we're going to look at promotional checklists and what processes we can put in place to make sure that we're getting our content in front of our audience.

Throughout this guide, we've touched on the importance of promoting content a few times. One of the biggest mistakes many people make is thinking that publishing content is that last stage of the process (which typically comes from being sick of the content they've created and not knowing how much energy they need to put into promotion). Often, there's also an over-reliance on our chosen platform's algorithms.

We want to challenge you to come up with a promotional checklist that you can use for the content you create.

Going forward, what you need to do is look at your different types and templates of content and create a promotional checklist for each. For now, let's reflect on the platforms we're using, the content types we've created and then work out how to give ourselves a thorough, manageable, and easy to follow checklist.

Checklist Template

In the Checklist Template, we've got our content title and two lists - direct and indirect forms of promotion. Going through this checklist every time you publish something means you then have a process that enables you to give your content the best chance of reaching and engaging with your audience.

Content Title: Long Form Blog Posts

....

In-Direct

Platform	Frequency: Quantity	per	Time-frame		Done
Facebook	3x	per	Week		☒
Tweet	5x	per	Week		☐
		per			☐
		per			☐
		per			☐
		per			☐
		per			☐

Direct

Platform	Frequency: Quantity	per	Time-frame		Done
Email	1000	per	Week		☒
		per			☐
		per			☐
		per			☐
		per			☐
		per			☐
		per			☐

Indirect Promotion

Examples of indirect promotion include things like posting your content on Facebook, Twitter and LinkedIn 3 times a week for the next 2 weeks. This frequency is achievable and manageable and something you can automate using tools like Content Cal, Sprout Social or Hootsuite.

Usually, we don't do this in a strategic way. It's more a case of "I've not promoted anything in a while, let me just share this and hopefully that's enough." Having this checklist in place will eliminate this sporadic, unplanned approach and provide structure to promoting your content.

Direct Promotion

You also want to make sure that you have direct promotional activities in place. A classic example of this will be sending an email (possibly using an email tool like Mail Chimp). The important thing here is deciding how many people to send this to and how often- it may be to the 1000 people on your email newsletter list once a week.

You also need to think about the platforms that have built-in direct messaging functions. For example, Facebook has Messenger, Instagram has DMs and LinkedIn has InMail. So, on your checklist, you might have 'to send an Instagram DM to 20 people'. To help you choose who these people are, have a look to see who's interacted with your latest content and say, "I saw that you liked my latest post. Here's a blog I've written, you might want to read it."

Using this checklist helps you to create time-boxed spaces in your schedule for promotional activities.

Think of a content type we spoke about earlier in our guide and take a few minutes to write down a few activities under direct promotion and indirect promotion, based on the platforms and channels you have available.

When looking at your list, you'll see that it looks and feels like a manageable process. You can also see the tangible value of following your checklist because you can see how they'll reach your audience.

Having a promotional checklist gives you a manageable toolkit to make sure that you get the reach and engagement for your content as and when you create it.

Chapter 11
The One Page Strategy

We're now in the final section of our guide! Looking back at the toolkits we've covered, you should see a cohesive strategy emerging- one that is manageable, clear and immediately actionable.

You'll see that, if you put 'building trust' at the heart of all your content, you will be able to welcome people to your business like never before; creating meaningful relationships that benefit both you and your clients.

You should also now understand how to educate, empathise with and entertain your audience while replicating your ideal face-to-face customer relationship through the language, style and design of your content.

These principles will change your approach to creating great quality content that lead to long-term, fruitful customer relationships.

One Page Strategy Planner

To wrap up our guide, we want to introduce you to the One Page Strategy Planner; a tool for documenting everything we've covered in one place. Think of it as a front cover to your content strategy.

(*template on the next page*)

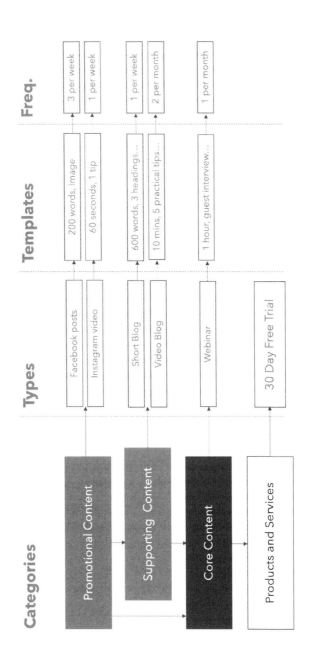

We've got the categories that we work with:

- Promotional content (to help people discover our brand)
- Supporting content (that helps us build trust and nurture relationship as well as demonstrate our expertise)
- Core content (that we use to convey strong value to potential customers, driving decision-making and buying behaviour)
- Products and services (which is what we're trying to funnel people through to)

Then, we've got content types. Are you going to create blogs, videos or LinkedIn posts? What are you creating and what platforms are you creating content for? What parameters are you going to create around those types of content to make sure that they're well-defined?

After that, we define those content types at an even deeper level by creating templates for them and that template is what moves us into the production part of our content strategy. Making sure you have templates in place before starting the creative process provides you with an amazing shortcut- it saves time and create positive constraints. So, how are you going to create efficiencies in your creative process?

Finally, we have frequency. This means looking at production as well as the promotion and thinking about how often you're going to commit to posting online.

When deciding how often you're going to produce and promote content, you also need to sense check against what's going to be manageable for you. If it's manageable, it's actionable, and only actionable goals will bring great results for your business.

Take a few minutes to write down some ideas on the One Page Strategy Planner, soak it all in and understand the decisions you've made, why you've made them and how you can start actioning them.

Your One Page Content Strategy:

You'll find a few here, so you can play around and see what works for you.

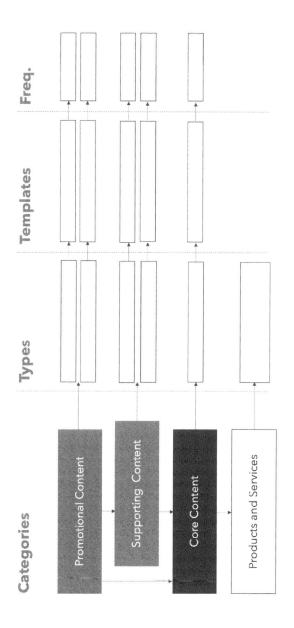

Categories   Types   Templates   Freq.

Promotional Content

Supporting Content

Core Content

Products and Services

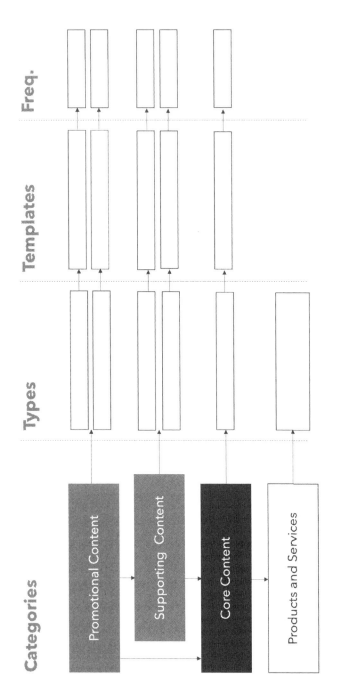

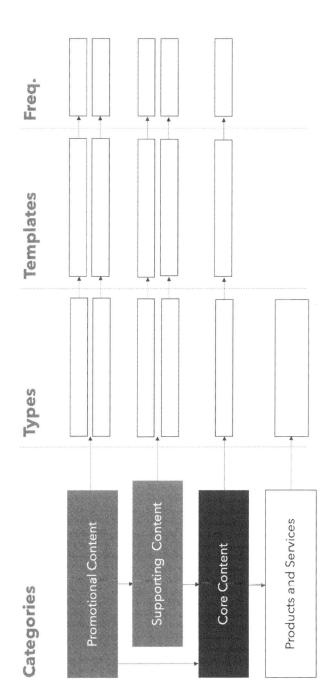

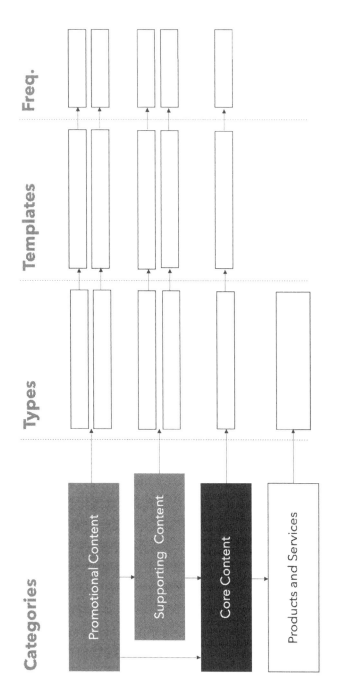

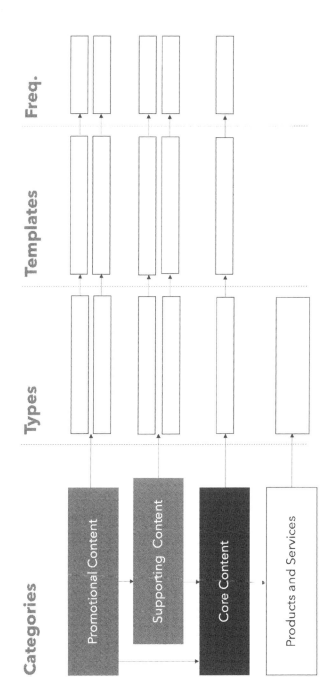

68

Closing Shot.

At the start of our guide, we spoke about the purpose of content; building trust, and how we demonstrate our brand's qualitative components, as well as how we humanize our business and turn our content into something unique that allows us to find and attract our ideal customers.

We then moved into planning; understanding our audience and what sorts of questions they may have and how we might answer those questions.

After that, we looked at the production of content. How do we approach the quality and the production of our content? Bearing in mind the 3 Es: education, empathy and entertainment and really understanding what our values are within each of those areas. We also covered creating templates so that we have really strong, reliable shortcuts in place for creating content.

Last but not least, we went through promoting content. Here we discussed making sure that we've selected the right platforms and channels for our brand, while appreciating our skills and confidence levels. Using our promotional checklist to make sure that once we've planned and created content we actually have something structured to rely on to create reach and engagement.

This brings us to the end of our guide. Thank you for taking the time to read this and, if you have any questions, get in touch with us.

We look forward to seeing your content and watching you build trusting, meaningful relationships with new customers through wonderful online content.

Trust at Scale
The Content Strategy, for Creative People

Written by:
Toby Moore

Published by:
Content Club™

Edited by:
Farrah Aslam and Julie Sydenham

Edition:
01 – 2021

For more learning visit
www.contentclub.io

Printed in Great Britain
by Amazon